To order additional copies of this book, contact:
Xlibris
AU TFN: 1 800 844 927 (Toll Free inside Australia)
AU Local: 0283 108 187 (+61 2 8310 8187 from outside Australia)
www.xlibris.com.au
Orders@Xlibris.com.au

ISBN: Softcover   978-1-6641-0435-8
          EBook   978-1-6641-0188-3

Print information available on the last page

Rev. date: 03/24/2021

CONTENTS

I bow to no mortal 2

God? 3

Equilibrium 4

New age slavery 8

United as a multiple 13

Is this enlightenment 15

Food of my soul, food for the earth 16

Trapped within the psyche 18

Drained veins and empty water holes 19

Dear Facebook 21

Nine-Five 24

I BOW TO NO MORTAL

I bow to no man
for what man is more pre-eminent
than the man next to him?
what man deserves respect when that man is decadent

I kneel to no man
for no man, in his heart
is greater than all men
not from the present, future or those from the start

I slouch my knees for none
who rest in the sphere of life
for they too rest as I rest
in this same sphere of strife

so, if we sleep and eat
love and enjoy
in the same atmosphere
then who is thee to command God's boy

2

GOD?

He shapes the particles of all existence
She is all and he is nothing, everywhere and no where
he built all that is seen and unseen with sheer persistence
She carried a burden no one could bare

He stands tall but never proud
She loves all but never lusts
his voice is soft, but his authority is loud
her heart is one where you may place your trust

We have written about him
identified him
but chances of being right are slim
and most depictions are grim

Se is indescribable for
how does one who has imperfection
explain the complex law
on one who is absolute perfection

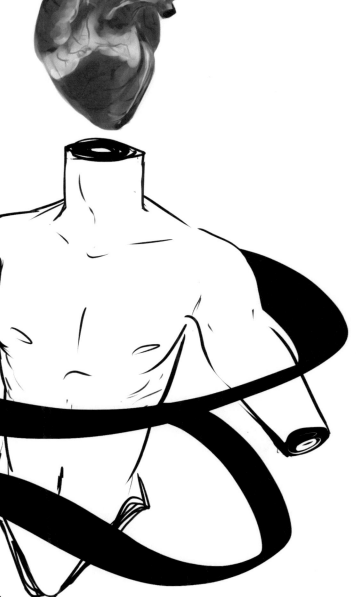

EQUILIBRIUM

When we harm the body of our mother
We harm the body of ourselves
Just as we harm the souls of our sister or brother
We harm the soul of ourselves

You see our flesh is not or own
Our spirit borrows it from the rich earth
And we wear it until it's death
Upon which it's returned to mother for another's birth

So, I say the love we feed the earth
Will be devoured by her land
And reincarnated for the birth of fresh life
Just as we were moulded by dirt and sand

With this I declare the hate and destruction
We feed our mother
Will be devoured by her land
And will abort the birth of our new-found sister and brother

So, I say love Mother Earth
Treat her peacefully and kind
And in perfect balance
Peace in the future we shall find

When we harm the body of our mother
We harm the body of ourselves
Just as we harm the souls of our sister or brother
We harm the soul of ourselves

You see our soul
Is made from the soul of our father
Upon our mortal death
We reform upon his altar

So, I say the joy we feed another's soul
Will be devoured as was the father's body
And so, upon it's reformed return
Love and joy it will embody

With this I declare the wrath and spite
We feed our family's will course through our father
And the riches of darkness
shall reign and prosper

So, I say look to our father
With faith and honour
For a soul we damage
May return as our son or daughter

When we harm the body of our mother
We harm the body of ourselves
Just as we harm the souls of our sister or brother
We harm the soul of ourselves

the father and mother rest in equilibrium
They breathe life and deliver birth
Deep into our souls
And far across every inch of the earth

5

So, I say the love we harbour in our hearts
And that courses through our veins
Will shine light upon the darkness
And shatter their shackles and chains

So, I declare the evil we harbour in our minds
And that courses through our veins
Will rip the light from our lands
And darkness will bind us in their chains

So, I say the love you hold for yourself
You should also hold for your mother and sisters
For if you don't your hate will burn you
To a putrid entity of scars and blisters

So, I say the love you hold for yourself
You should also hold for your father and brothers
For if your pride and wrath rule your heart
You'll bring all the world to suffer

6

A WORLD IN TROUBLE

Ashes to ashes
Castles fallen to rubble
Severe car crashes
A world in trouble

H2O interference
Layers peeling away
An earth of experience
Causing an extinction in a day

Protectors attempted meddling
Have mutated to greedy parasites
To their own demise they're peddling
For she stands her ground and fights

Ending in a prophecy
One or another
It doesn't matter about the hypocrisy
All that matters is to love one another

NEW AGE SLAVERY

Dictators free themselves but imprison the people
Thriving off their slavery
To build the steps of their steeple
Remaining innocent with sly knavery

A time not so short of ours
Slave masters owned the masses
They herded us like cows
But now they hide behind the fasces

What was once thought eradicated
Has only succumbed to evolution
The mind set of slavery has integrated
With the workers constitution

We may not kneel to the whip's authority
But we are thralls to classical conditioning
Slaves to the master minds of psychology
And money has caused our freedoms partitioning

The exact time of our freedom is calculated
Nine to three, nine to five, twenty-four seven
Our structure of freedom has been fabricated
And slavers create hell disguised as heaven

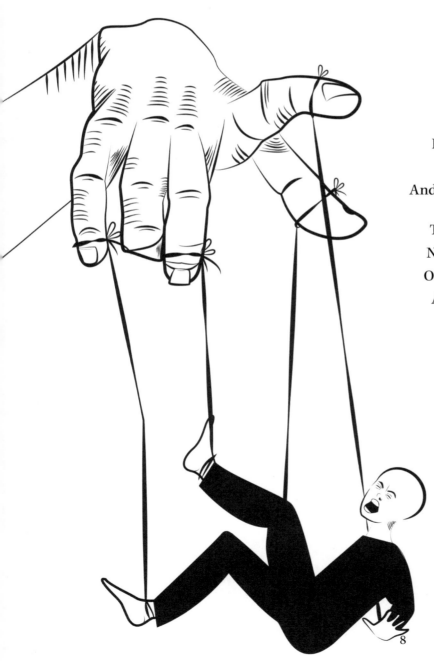

Inch by inch we lose more of our autonomy
From time to thoughts to mortality from divine
And being a slave is portrayed as being set free
As quoted by Wittgenstein

We're placed in an individualistic room
With an inward opening door, unlocked
And we've been led to assume
That the pushed door is blocked

Our essence is being drained
To the point of becoming an automated zombie
Freedom from whips and chains we may have gained
But shackles restrict our psyche

Now a wise man once said
There is no greater victory than to die a freeman
So, before you lay with death in her bed
Make sure you achieve liberation in your lifespan

TO DIE ALONE

Dad can we talk
I have an issue that I need to express
I think it's best if we take a walk
As the fresh air will relieve some stress

Dad I really worry
Your ticks are slowing down on your clock
And I have to say sorry
But it gets me that you won't listen to the doc

You're a man and an adult
You should be taking responsibility
Now it pains me, and I don't mean to insult
But you need to move to a housing facility

Son you are right death is around the corner
But I'm a man who's at peace with death
He's no longer a foreigner
But I won't be caught waiting for my last breath

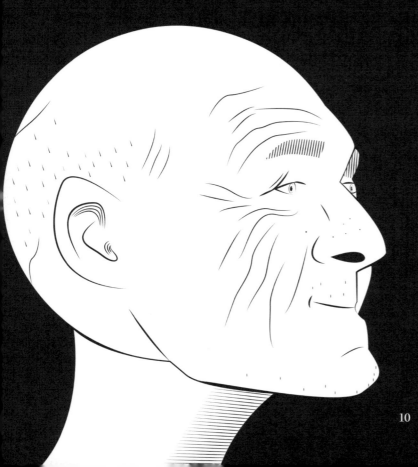

Son I've never been a man of pharmaceuticals
Their drugs fill your mind making you complacent
Herding your thoughts into a cubical
I'm sorry son but I don't want be a trapped patient

I'm a man harbouring a mind wild and free
I always have and always will
I'm old and carefree
And will keep doing so until my heart stands still

Please dad I implore
Your recklessness causes me stress
And your someone I adore
There's no one left for you to impress

I can't keep living like this
Running to your every aid
Because you choose to remiss
I don't think I can continue this charade

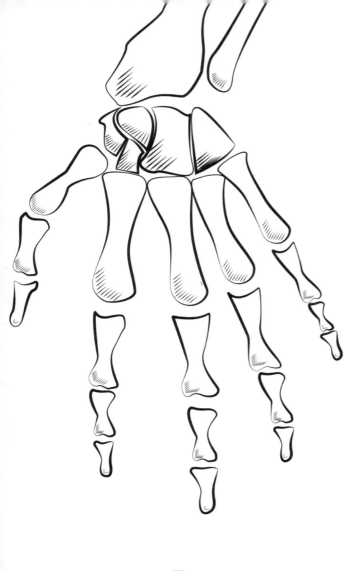

Son my actions are never to impress
I'm a man comfortable in his skin
Your words hurt but I love you non the less
For you are my kin

But I never asked you to take this responsibility
for me to be your priority
but I desire amicability
though I am my own authority

It's final it's settled
I've made up my mind
Without a shred of being nettled
I define the soul that is mine until my life's resigned

But dad...
Son as you said I'm an adult
And I know my decision makes you sad
But I prefer to die with emotions of exult

Than spend my days confined to
meds and a small room
I don't expect you to understand
Just know my love for you will always bloom
But I'll decide where I end in God's plan

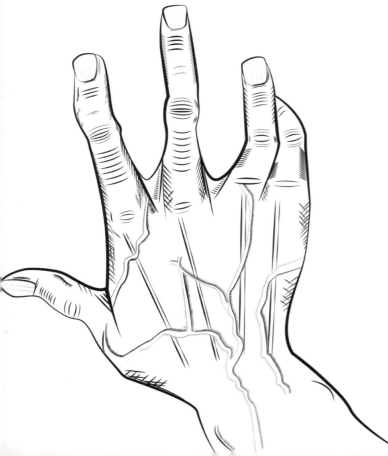

UNITED AS A MULTIPLE

Bend the will of the mind
To enslave all of man kind
Dissolve actuality
To reconstruct a Utopian reality

Dress the wolves as sheep
To devour any that aren't asleep
Crush the words of truth
With any and all false proof

Hide behind your mirrors and smoke
While you allow generations to soak
In your whispered fable
Feeding them putrid ideologies from the table

Nail the free to planks of wood
Rip apart all of those who could
Break the chains of the oppressed
Keep the keys of truth veiled and suppressed

Create an ant farm
To keep the storm calm
Create ticking clocks
Hinging all in psychological locks

Piles upon piles
To you we are just case files
Cattle off for the kill
To raise the pile of your forged bill

Freedom is taught but never reached
Slavery is achieved but never preached
We crave social unicity
But are taught to be a singular entity

You fear the knowledge of equality, all as one
So you conjure all to live under your rule of thumb
Severing the chains of the United
Clouding our sight, keeping us blind sighted

Forever we are slaves to oppression
Never freeing our intelligent expressions
Waiting for one to set us free
But for all to be free one we all must be

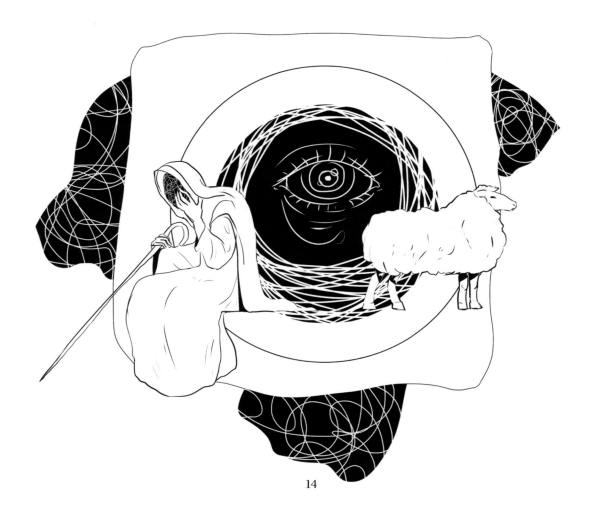

IS THIS ENLIGHTENMENT

We're born from the earth's perfection

But from birth where pushed in the wind's direction

We're born into a world of endless dreams

But the taller one grows the harder one leans

To the winds ever growing momentum

though very, few only some

Stop amidst the crowds' grind

to look deep inside to try and find

Who they really are

They stop looking down and notice the stars

Their perspective becomes third person

Realisation of the devil's coercion

Fills their once empty void of consciousness

A man now autonomous

Deep searching of the galaxy

Removes the veil of reality

Eyes now see crystal clear

And doubts of spirituality disappear

A man once herded like a cow

Paid minimum wage for the field he ploughed

Now makes a shift in belief

No more is he just a hunk of beef

He turns one eighty degree in his herd

Whispers grip his ears saying he's absurd

But deaf to the blind

He leaves his past behind

He walks away from the devil's claws

His soul begins to reform and restore

God, arms open embraces him with excitement

FOOD OF MY SOUL, FOOD FOR THE EARTH

Death upon death, a life celebrated
Pointless solitude built to decay
Holy soil, food for the soul desecrated
Spirits of memory trapped, so respects we can pay

Forrest of concrete infesting sacred land
Harbouring what rightfully belongs to Mother Earth
Rich comfort for dirt and sand
When such richness could breathe life's birth

So, as I am carried away on deaths steed
And I pass from the mother and am received by the father
I shall be buried with the only possession of a seed
So, life rooted in my death can be provided for another

I desire no comfort of a casket
For my body is only nutrients for creation
Mother Earth will not receive me in a wastebasket
I shall be woven into life's foundation

There will be no death upon mine
No branch broken and no tree shall fall
There will be no stone marking my shrine
Only a seed which will grow tall

Through this tree I shall remain alive
As I dissolve into mother earths body
The tree of my essence shall thrive
And through this tree my memories shall embody

Alone in a field or one amidst a forest
I shall provide life from my quietus
My body shall begin the reforest
As my soul rest with Jesus

TRAPPED WITHIN THE PSYCHE

We as a community
Need to express all we harbour inside
All of our beauty and impurity
Needs to be expressed in one we confide

For if we spend long hours with our internalized demon and angel
We become lost in our conscious thought stream
Which can be increasingly baneful
As our nightmares can infest our day dream

Introspection is a grand quality
The ability to talk to entities
That live subconsciously
Though insanity is born from sanity and we may lose our identities

So as an individual psyche
One must become part of a multiple
To express such emotions to their community
Or your soul can easily become destructible

Always hold on to your individualistic value
But never fear external expression
Make sure to your essence remain true
And always externalize what's internalized to avoid great depression

DRAINED VEINS AND EMPTY WATER HOLES

Wolves white and black as night
Wear sheep skins to trade souls out of sight
What was once water is blood on my hands
I drink the essence of ancestral lands

Herds of lambs trapped in paddocks
Souls in chains, linked with padlocks
Meat without spirits, food for the wolf
The damned awaiting they're Beowulf

Drained veins and empty water holes
Plague the lands of ancestors' souls
Genocide infested ideologies
creating and building colonies

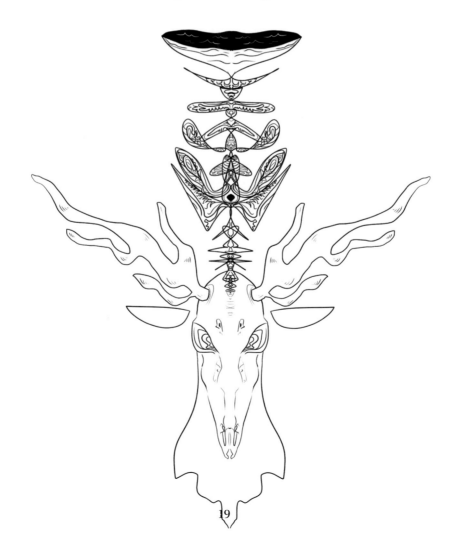

UNWARRANTED

Moments spent in bliss
Or in grim solitude meditating
While demon minds come to parti-pris
Removing the process of equating

An issue I see quotidian
Roused by the mundane and unperceptive
For venom corrodes our hearts left by the ophidian
Conjuring a perfect loving connection contraceptive

To many philosophers read books by their bound leather
Never turning a page to see what the author has to say
So, mutes sign language to the deaf to lead the blind together
And all who feel are left to be the wolf's prey

Wolfs eat sheep and man plays judge
Snakes whisper lies and man plays executioner
we succumb all too quick to begrudge
Our fellow man's Lucifer

Yet the presence of demon's wear halos in these moments
And false assumptions seep into the witness's eyes
As if they don't hold their own atonements
Glaring down noses believing they're closer to heavens skies

Yet Shepherds beat down foxes and wolves
In hopes that balance is equated
And we cut off horse hooves
To glue peace and chaos so balance can be created

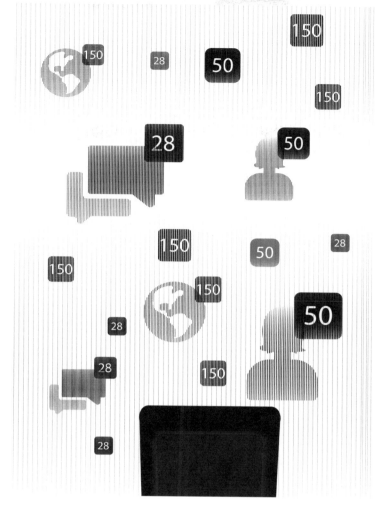

DEAR FACEBOOK

Dear Facebook,
you promise popularity you promise friends
But no matter the number I find myself alone in the end
You give many what they want, yet many useless desire
You feed our hunger with products soon to expire

Dear Facebook,
you surround me with many faces
Though no matter the number we're never in the same places
You cook food for the tasteless
And create souls for the faceless

Dear Facebook,
You leave us free in the confines of subliminal messaging
Thoughts written in sentences succumb to your editing
Separations caused by public scrutiny
Yet what you promise is unity

Dear Facebook,
You promise freedom of expression
Yet we still see increasing numbers of depression
You promise people connection
In a platform desensitised to affection

Dear Facebook,
I ask what it is you teach our youth?
With so many claiming they know the truth
Yet you sit and sleuth
Crediting those you deem fit with proof

Dear Facebook,
Your concept is fruitful
Yet in controversial matters you need to remain neutral
And we as a society who thinks free
Need to build a loving and caring community

TO FEAST UPON CULTURE

Tears roll down the face of a child less mother
For her child has been aborted before her eyes
By those who claim to be her brother
The snakes that whisper to her lies

The seed of her future has been devoured by the beast
And now the heir to her precious heart
Has become the blackened doves feast
A bloody mess, mutilated and torn apart

A cry bellowed from the belly of a childless father
For his child has been aborted before his eyes
By he who claims to be his forefather
The snakes that whisper to him lies

The seed of his future has been devoured by the beast
And now the heir to his fragile soul
Has become the white Ravens feast
A horror buried deep in the graves hole

Grieving sobs breathe from a sibling-less sister
For her brother was murdered before her eyes
By the one who claims to be the freedom oppressing resister
The snakes that whisper to her lies

The roots of her future has been devoured by the beast
And now the guardian of her pure heart
Has become the wolves feast
Blood ingurgitated for black art

A breath of despair wails from a sibling-less brother
For his sister was murdered before his eyes
By she who claims to be his mother
The snakes that whispers to him lies

The roots of his future has been devoured by the beast
And now the guardian of his growing soul
Has become the leeches feast
The innocent slaughtered or enslaved by mind control

NINE-FIVE

We walk idly with the grey crowd
Ravens circling above and vultures licking lips
But we continue to walk in oppression to make someone proud
Marching towards already filled crypts

Construction of time to control our life
Governments formed to control our rights
The perfect life is to have three kids and a wife
And to hide all imperfection until they turn off the lights

Alarm bells toll before the sun at seven
To wake us up for breakfast
We go to work and have lunch at eleven
Before going home at eight to rest

Alarm bells toll before the sun at seven
And we are awoken in a zombie state
Wishing we could close our eyes and dream of heaven
But we can't because if we do, we'll be late

So we pick up our ball and chain of oppression
Walking towards the man that holds our worth
Slowly being conditioned to depression
As we realise our value is dearth